Nonfiction – 20,666 words

THE LOVE WITHIN

by

Tamara Dalton

FOREWORD

By Dylan Ward

"When you are so spiritually

disconnected to yourself, to your higher

power, and to the God within, you become

a dry shell."

Dalton grew up as a young girl in a comfortable but strict

household in Haiti. Her self-worth was deeply affected by the lack

of affection from her parents. There is even suspicion of domestic

violence between them. All of this instilled a lifelong struggled

within Dalton to find love and happiness with others, as she

assimilated in American culture, achieved a career in nursing, and

married and divorced men in abusive relationships. Dreams and

goals were altered by what Dalton refers to as "wrong turns" on her

path through adulthood. After experiencing a spiritual awakening,

she discovered a newfound mental and physical strength from the

"godly power within" to escape the continuous abuse in a life

entrapped by low self-worth.

Writing about the inspirations she found during dark times

of her life, Dalton shares her painful, personal story of how she

empowered herself with her faith in God to find new purpose and

meanings. Her self-help book serves as both a memoir and

support for others facing similar crises. What Dalton considered

as her humanitarian efforts to help others to be whole again is

partially attained through this book that is both therapeutic and

enlightening. It reads like an autobiography but is structured as a resource book, too. Each chapter ends with guidance questions for discussion and reflection. Also included is a Bonus Workbook of her Three R's Program with tips and opportunities to help plan a course of action for obtaining a life used to the fullest. It is a good read for those seeking to better themselves and let go of the fears that otherwise stunt their passage to higher self and happiness.

Although every precaution has been taken to verify the accuracy of the information contained herein, the author and publisher

assume no responsibility for any errors or omissions. No liability

is assumed for damages that may result from the use of

information contained within.

ISBN-13: 9780692063071

ISBN-10: 0692063072

Printed in the United States of America

YOU ARE LOVELY

God Designed You That Way

TamaraLifeCoach.com

CONTENTS

Chapter 1   Feeling Empty Inside

Chapter 2   Growing Up on the Island

Chapter 3   Adapting to a New Environment

Chapter 4   Shattered Dream and Crumbling Plans

Chapter 5   My First Marriage, Looking for Stability

Chapter 6   Moving to Florida for a Change

Chapter 7   Education Was Always on my Mind

Chapter 8   Looking for Love Again

Chapter 9   Low Self-Esteem Leads to Poor Decisions

Chapter 10 Spiritual Aspect of Life

Chapter 11 Surrender, Let in God, Let God, and Move on

Chapter 12 Quest for Happiness

                 The Love Within Bonus Workbook

                 Four Steps to Finding Your Life's Purpose

PREFACE

I will give thanks to you because I

have been so amazingly and miraculously

made. Your works are miraculous, and

my soul is fully aware of this.

Psalm 139:14

The Love Within is a book about making wrong turns in your life and then getting back on the right track to love yourself again through the power of the Almighty. It will inspire you to dig a little deeper into your own heart to find the love, joy, happiness, and success you so greatly deserve. Life can get hard when you're driving down a road on the wrong path. For me, it was searching to find a positive lifestyle. However, I kept falling back into the same old negative types of relationships and patterns with people who were not going in the same direction I wanted.

During one of the darkest times of my life, I discovered the secret that inspired me and helped revitalize my life. This small voice inside me saved me and brought me to the light. I wrote this book for others to share the experience, knowledge, and wisdom I learned from making those wrong turns. You, too, can use the godly power within to rejuvenate your life. You will gain wisdom as you discover your soul and life's purpose, which will move you to achieve your most-impossible dreams.

ACKNOWLEDGMENT

I would like to thank God for giving me the strength and enlightening me in my darkest time and for never forsaking me. I want to thank my children for being my solid rock and for being the very best children any parent could've asked for. My sons, Mitchell Dalton, Brandon Dalton, Daniel Dalton, and Nathan

Nunez—I love you boys so much.

I would like to thank my mother for being the strongest woman I ever knew and for teaching me about God when I was growing up. Also, my father, for always ensuring we were in excellent schools when I was growing up in Haiti and for instilling the value of education in us.

I'm also thankful for my siblings: Chantal, Ruth, Rutha, Gurlaine, Annette, and my brother Gasner, nephews and nieces for being there for me in your own way. I would also like to thank my church pastor, Pat, for being a good spiritual advisor. I'd like to thank all my FB friends and fans for their support. Also, thanks to Mrs. Luz Lopez, Beth Torlano, and my spiritual sis Vivian Bradley and Ruby Etorna. You guys are the best.

A big shout-out to Karen Gillman with On Point Executive Center for a great book cover and for being supportive of my endeavors, Melissa Rodriguez, thank you girl for being a good longtime friend, Michael Bench, my videographer and to my photographer Rick Tauceda and my publicist Courtnie Gilmour for all your good work and support.

And we know that for those who love God, all things work together for good, for those who are called according to his purpose.

Romans 8:28

No, in all these things we are more
than conquerors through Him who loved
us. For I am sure that neither death nor
life, nor angels nor rulers, nor things
present nor things to come, nor powers,
nor height nor depth, nor anything else in

all creation, will be able to separate us

from the love of God in Christ Jesus our

Lord.

Romans 8:37-39

CHAPTER ONE

Feeling Empty

I made a few wrong turns in life by looking for love in all the wrong places, and that caused me to trust the wrong people with my heart. What I really needed to do was find the love of God within myself. My Creator has never forsaken me when I was on the wrong path or while I learned from my mistakes. I only needed reach inside myself to find the divine power within during the moments I felt alone. I knew returning to God could help me find myself, yet I didn't do it, because I was so lost inside. I wanted and needed someone to love me and share my life. I needed the love of an individual instead of the real love of my Heavenly Father. My self-esteem was depressed from feeling so empty inside.

Growing up in a house where hugs, kisses, and affection were never displayed played a part in my low self-esteem. My parents loved us, but that was how they were raised. They displayed their love through actions, such as ensuring we had a place to live, nourishing food, and good clothes. Education was a must. We never missed going to church on Sunday. Church was a big deal but going to church as a routine isn't enough to make young children understand the true meaning of God. I knew my parents loved me, but the lack of affection left me always wanting to be loved by others.

My parents were very strict with us, which was a good thing in some ways, because we never got into trouble, tried drugs, or drank alcohol. However, my parents created a negative family lifestyle and home life with constant fights, arguments, and yelling between them. It never occurred to me until much later in life that what happened in my life as a child or growing up had to do with the way I was raised. Self-development is very important, and I didn't know how to connect to or with my inner self and soul. I also didn't know how to meditate on God's Word, pray, or understand I had spiritual needs. I had poor interpersonal communication skills, which deal with others outside the self, and I had poor intrapersonal communication skills, which deal with the internal self. I had no self-esteem, no idea how or to whom I should reach for help.

To understand low self-esteem, we must first understand the word. According to the *Collins Thesaurus of the English Language, Complete and Unabridged Second Edition* (2002), self-esteem is self-love, self-reliance, self-pride, self-respect, self-assurance, courage, and confidence. What is low self-esteem? It is the opposite, the absence of all those great words. Why do some people have high self-esteem and others have low self-esteem? People don't just grow up and purposely choose to look down on themselves.

There are many reasons why someone ends up with low self-image. For me, it wasn't something my parents knew how to cultivate in us. If no one introduces knowledge to a person about the human body, he or she might never learn how to help himself develop personally.

Understanding Our Self-Esteem

Self-esteem is the value and worth you assign to yourself. It affects how you treat yourself and how you let others treat you. Self-esteem could be generalized, or it could be specific to one aspect or area of your life. For example, you may have low self-esteem about your talents and abilities. Usually, those who come from negative backgrounds, as I mentioned earlier, will have low self-esteem in various areas of their lives. It influences their core beliefs, which directly influence how they perceive themselves and others. Subsequently, it influences their lifestyle choices, decision-making skills, and how people interact with them. It's crucial to understand what self-esteem is and how those fundamental concepts form a person's paradigm and guide one's behavior.

Self-esteem is influenced by self-efficacy and self-concept. Self-efficacy is the belief one has about accomplishing an objective and depends on perceptions of one's competence. Self-concept is the belief of how a person perceives and describes himself. It includes core beliefs about respect, love, giving, receiving, health, money and riches, and dreams—what someone does or does not deserve. People with low self-esteem have distorted self-concepts and poor perceptions regarding their self-efficacy. Normally, such a belief isn't a person's fault. It's often created by lack of awareness of self. When you shine the light of awareness on yourself, you see and realize what a magnificent being you are. As a result, people start developing self-compassion and learn to love themselves more.

Factors That Have a Negative Impact on Self-Esteem

There are several reasons why someone may have low self-esteem. For me, it was being physically and emotionally neglected by my parents, facing trauma and abuse, and living in a stigmatized society in Haiti.   Many factors can lead to low self-esteem, including:

- Social, emotional, sexual, or physical abuse
- Being bullied or facing excessive pressure to live up to expectation as a child or an adult
- Feeling socially isolated and lonely within the surrounding environment.
- Facing loss and going through the bereavement process.
- Being faced with trauma in any form can lead to stress disorder and post-traumatic stress disorder, particularly when you aren't able to cope with the trauma and lack the social support necessary to get through the trauma.
- When you face the dilemma of conforming to norms and values due to peer pressure but don't necessarily agree with them.
- Suffering from any form of physical or mental ailment or health concerns.

- Having to live in a poverty-stricken household, neighborhood, or society.
- Feeling lost due to not being able to connect with and put your trust in God. You become dependent on people and stop relying on God and don't ask for help from the Almighty.

Summary

Childhood memories and bonds with your parents hold great importance in our lives. They impact your current self positively, negatively, or both. Realizing the memories, we can clearly recall acts as pathways to a better understanding of our inner lives and positive traits, as well as our suffering.

Understanding self-esteem is crucial to starting the inner journey of self-understanding, self-compassion, and self-love. Recall what you read in this chapter. What is self-esteem? How is it often affected in daily life? Why should you proactively address it?

Psychological trauma and witnessing any act of terror or pain can lead to failure, rejection, low-self-esteem, guilt, loneliness, brooding, and rumination. These are emotional and psychological hurts. They leave you feeling empty and longing for love. Like any physical hurt, they need to be tended.

Chapter Review

I had loving parents. They meant well, but they didn't know how to connect with me at an emotional level, which left me sad and lonely.

What about you? How did you feel growing up?

Did you ever feel empty inside when you were growing up?

Were you able to express your feelings to your parents without fear?

Do you believe that the decisions you made in life were impacted by the environment in which you grew up?

Exercises

1. Family exercise during dinner: State one good thing you love about each other.

2. Form a family circle as a ritual and hug each other.

3. Write a note or letter to your parents expressing how you felt during your childhood and let the ink of the letter wash away in the ocean.

4. Draw a good memory from your childhood and frame it in your home.

As long as you're chasing the ghosts
of your past, you can never fully embrace
your future.

Oprah Winfrey

You shall teach them diligently to
your children and shall talk of them when
you sit in your house, and when you walk
by the way, and when you lie down, and
when you rise.

Deuteronomy 6:7 (ESV)

CHAPTER TWO

Growing Up on the Island

I grew up in Haiti, a small island beside the Dominican
Republic. Haiti was a nice place back then, but our parents were
very strict. They didn't allow us to go outside the house unless it
was for school, then someone had to take us and bring us back

home.

In Haiti, it's said there's no such thing as the middle class. However, our family was middle class. We weren't rich or poor. If my parents were struggling, they hid it very well, because they always wanted us to have a good life, especially my mother. A courageous woman, she would do anything to make sure we were comfortable. For instance, she entered the United States to give my siblings and me a secure, concrete future.

My mother had seven children when she arrived in the United States. She came to America legally and had a traveling visa to go back and forth from Haiti to the U.S. as a merchant.

She left us in Haiti with our father and traveled to the U.S. to find work. Father stayed home to care for us while Mother was away. When Jean-Claude Duvalier, President of Haiti, a dictator, was forced out of power, the country went into an uproar. Haiti began changing for the worst.

One of the things I most admired about Mother was her determination to bring all her children to the United States. She decided to stop traveling back and forth to America. Instead, she remained there, worked hard, saved all her money, and brought her family to the United States. I realize now she wanted a better life for us. She knew there were more opportunities in the world besides the tough lifestyle we had in Haiti. She didn't like the changes in Haiti and knew getting us out was our only chance for a better future.

She worked hard as a dry cleaner for long hours, saving all the money she earned. She was very smart with money. I believe that's where I inherited watching and tracking the way I spend my own hard-earned money, too. Soon, Mother met a woman who told her she could bring all her children to the United States, but it came with a price.

Mother paid the woman a lump sum, emptying her savings account to bring us all to the States for a better life. A good mother does anything to protect her children, hoping their future will be better than hers. Mother didn't bat an eye when the offer came. She paid the entire sum without borrowing from anyone, bringing us to America safely. I was very glad she did. I never knew what would have happened to me if I stayed in Haiti during those difficult times.

Even though I knew Mother loved me by her nonverbal gestures of working hard and being a great provider, there was still a lack of emotional support when I grew up. The lack of her presence left me sad and depressed. During my childhood and teen years, I always felt lonely, sad, and alone in the world, especially since we were left with my father, a very distant person who never showed anger.

I began studying him in fear, wondering what happened in his life that diminished his self-worth and left him so damaged. I vowed one day, I'd have my own family and would make sure they grew up with love, affection, and compassion from two good and loving parents. I didn't realize that children who witness domestic violence suffer emotional and psychological trauma.

Many times, such children carry deep internal scars from the impact of living in a household dominated by tension and fear. Those children usually end up in abusive relationships themselves.

I always felt traumatized, lonely, fearful, and insecure. Since I was good at hiding my feelings from others, people saw me as

happy and carefree. If only they had seen what was going on
inside my soul and how it screamed for help. In Haitian culture,
crying was for the weak and faint of heart. If a child expressed
such fears to her parents, it was looked upon as a sign of
disrespect and lack of gratitude to them.

My background and the way I was raised impacted my life
and my decisions. No matter how clear my intentions were to do
well in life, there was always a but. According to
EffectivePhilanthropy.com, an individual's behavior and health,
family life, learning environment, and socioeconomic environment
influence his or her behavior as an adult. Yes, all face choices in
life, and we can't blame our parents for poor choices. When we
were young, our parents made choices for us. It's not until
someone reaches the age of twenty-one (in America) that he or she
is considered grown and a legal adult, able to manage his or her
affairs. However, the environmental factor plays a big role in how
we act, react, choose, and think when finding a domestic partner.
Growing up, even when I knew I wanted a better family life than
what my parents had, I subconsciously wanted the same thing,

because that was all I knew.

Symptoms of Low Self-Esteem

Here are some common signs and indicators of people with low self-esteem.

- You always compare yourself to others who may have seemingly happy lives. When you start comparing yourself with others who have a better life than yours, instead of looking at those who might be in worse conditions than yours, you're bound to become trapped in a vicious cycle of low-self-esteem and will make life decisions accordingly.
- You put yourself down constantly and believe you deserve the worst. When something good comes along, you tend to sabotage it, because your core belief is that you don't deserve anything good in your life.
- Those with low self-esteem experience depression, anxiety, and a feeling of being judged by others based on perceived flaws.

- You think and say negative things about yourself constantly. The universe picks up on those signals and starts to resonate with them. You begin to attract negative people who pull you down further toward low self-esteem.

- You become dependent on people who disrespect you and stay away from prayers and putting your trust in God. Instead the people around you pull you back into negativity and low self-esteem.

- You surround yourself with negative thinking, negative talk, and negative people, becoming more distant from God, until you suffer from an inferiority complex.

Summary

Environment plays a crucial role in how we develop our self-image, think of ourselves, and what we think we deserve and are capable of. It trains the subconscious to accept or reject certain things, including what we can have in life.

To find inner peace, it's crucial to understand your limiting beliefs and subconscious programming, then actively change it.

Chapter Review

Who are you? Think about your life growing up. Did you struggle with low self-esteem?

How was your home life while you grew up? Be honest with yourself, because the way you interacted with your family leaves a lasting effect on your brain. You must learn how to manage the scares, thoughts, and the videos in your mind left from years of pain, fear, or sadness. You must release these old thoughts to find the love within yourself, because the old will block the new from being revealed and attracted to you.

Who am I?

Maybe you were happy growing up, but you still must remember as many details as possible. This will help you move forward to find new, exciting ways to love yourself.

Am I happy inside? What random thoughts do you allow to take control of your life?

List your positive qualities and your shortcomings.

Shortcomings   Positive Qualities

Try to minimize one shortcoming for a month.

It's time to find inner peace by letting go of people who are holding your self-love from you.

- Hold a balloon for each bitter memory or thought you have.
- Speak your mind, pretending the person is next to you, then release the balloon into the air. Visualize the scenario while making peace and letting go of the feeling after acknowledging it.

- Let go of all the bitter thoughts.

- On the second page of the review of Chapter 2, note down thoughts and the emotion you feel with those thoughts.

- Realize what you want and would love to have in your life. Don't worry about how it would be possible. Think of what you'd love to have in your relationships, current health, professional life, money, and free time. Free your mind of all obstacles and think. List the answers.

> When you recover or discover
> something that nourishes your soul and
> brings joy, care enough about yourself to
> make room for it in your life.
>
> Jean Shinoda Bolen

FAMILY

Our Refuge from the Storm

Our Link from the Past

Our Bridge to the Future

CHAPTER THREE

Adapting to a New Environment

I moved from Haiti to the United States when I was fifteen. I didn't speak English, just French and Creole, but the lack of spoken English didn't stop me from fitting in right away with the American people. I felt right at home, though there were challenges with things I'd never seen before.

I had my first pizza in America and ate it with a spoon. My classmates laughed and made fun of me. Obviously, there were things to work on while I adapted to American culture.

When I arrived, I felt instantly connected to the country. I told myself, *this is home.* I can still say that today. America is my home. Even before I became an American citizen, in my heart, I knew America was my home. I knew I would stay here and live a daily dream. Perhaps my lack of connection with Haiti had to do with the fact I was never outside my house except to go to school. Maybe it was due to my clouded understanding of Haitian culture. In any case, my connection was always with the United States.

Although I love America and enjoy living here, I know who I am, and I keep some of my cultural traits. I still believe in cooking for my husband. I don't like to cook, but I always found myself cooking when I was married.

I'm always verbal about where I'm from and who I am as an island woman. I'm very proud of where I came from. Unfortunately, Haiti faces many obstacles. The 7.0 earthquake in

2010 left the country in extreme poverty, and it continues to be the poorest country in the Western Hemisphere. However, Haiti was also the first Black country in the Western Hemisphere, gaining its independence on January 1, 1804, and abolishing slavery.

I'm proud to be Haitian. I don't keep up with the news from Haiti, because it is rarely good, and that can be unbearable to me. I try to stay focused on the positive. My goal is eventually to do charitable work there.

Once I came to the United States, I left my memories of Haiti behind. My focus was to make the best out of my life and be productive here.

> Occasionally God
> Rips aside the veil,
> And you begin to see
> This very fact:
>
> All things happen for you.
> All things.

Every...thing

Is knit together.

Tim Keller

Summary

Challenges and adversity are opportunities to understand your own self and move toward a better future.

Accepting the challenge as an opportunity is the first step toward using it as a new beginning to start fresh with a clean slate. Your past plays no role in what you can do in the future unless you let it.

Take an honest look at your current life and understand whatever has happened in the past was needed to make you who you are, and to prepare you for what you need to do now.

We must recognize when opportunities are offered and learn to recognize and avail ourselves of them with full potential and positivity.

Learning to be flexible and adaptable to a new environment

is important while staying connected to your roots and where you came from.

Chapter Review

Write down some of the challenges you face today. What are the solutions that can help you make the right choices?

What was a life-changing event you went through? What were your struggles? How did you overcome those difficult times? Think about the events that made you who you are today and how you were able to conquer them.

Create a collage or a scrapbook representing your struggles and how you overcame them. Create a pictorial form of the story.

When we least expect it,

Life sets us a challenge to test

Our courage and willingness to change.

                         Pailo Coelho

Trust in the Lord with all your heart

and lean not on your own understanding;

in all your ways submit to him, and he will

make your paths straight.

Psalms 3:5-6 (NIV)

CHAPTER FOUR

Shattered Dream and Crumbled Plans

No matter what was going on in our household when I was growing up, my parents enforced our getting an education. I always wanted to be educated. My parents encouraged this. Education was embedded in my mind. One of my goals was to work in the medical field.

When I was seven-years old, I was hit by a truck and was severely injured. The nurses, doctors, and therapists helped me tremendously to recover fully. Due to that terrible experience, I began to consider a medical career when I was in high school. I knew when I graduated with a diploma that I would go straight to college to become a doctor.

Once again, I had no clue my life would turn out to be a series of obstacles, but Proverbs 16:1-3 (ESV) says, *the plans of the heart belong to man, but the answer of the tongue is from the Lord. All the ways of a man are pure in his own eyes, but the Lord weighs the spirit. Commit your work to the Lord, and your plans will be established.*

> They say knowledge is power. I say knowledge is freedom.
>
> Coach Tamara

I wanted a family of my own and focused on being happy without knowing the necessary ingredients to be happy. I was so focused and afraid of having a life like that of my parents, I ended up making wrong turns and a series of mistakes. All along, my focus should have been on God.

As God stated in Psalms 37:4 (ESV), *Delight yourself in the Lord, and He will give you the desires of your heart.*

I thought everything was going great. Life was good, and I didn't think of God at all. The minute an individual puts God last and relies on himself or herself, he or she will fall, because God is the master of our lives, every breath we take. Without Him, we are nothing, and nothing can be done right.

I graduated from high school and hadn't changed my mind about attending college and becoming a doctor. My mother also filed for our green card. It was supposed to arrive before I graduated high school.

As I completed my college education, we received bad news. I would not receive a green card due to issues with immigration when I entered the country. I was already in deportation to return to Haiti. Terrified, I was unable to see myself living there again.

Instead of relying on God, praying, and meditating, I again

relied on myself—another mistake, but such things can happen to anyone when we stop believing God.

Going back to Haiti wasn't part of my plan, and it wasn't an option for me. The reality of returning to Haiti started to sink in. I felt I had no choice but to marry an American, which wasn't part of my plan, either. My goal was to go to school, get an education first, then meet Mr. Right, have two children, and live happily ever after.

That all changed in a heartbeat. I had to do something fast. When you act based on frustration, you're heading for serious trouble.

Core Beliefs and Self-Esteem

Each of us has a set of core beliefs that guide every decision we make and affect how we perceive the world around us. Negative and destructive core beliefs take away your trust in God and influence the way you perceive yourself and others. This adds to uncertainty, anxiety, and often depression.

It's important to change your core beliefs and not let them be influenced by past negative experiences or your current situation. Trust yourself and God and find peace within yourself that you can change yourself and your situation. Use your God-given power to find your inner strength and build your self-esteem.

The moment you start to respect yourself, love yourself, and embrace God, you'll start seeing things differently. You must strive toward being exactly what you want to be. To have high self-esteem, you must strive toward it by becoming aware of your core beliefs, changing your mindset, and breaking free of your negative situation. When you do, you'll move toward a beautiful state of bliss, a positive and healthy self-esteem.

Components of Positive Self-Esteem

To change your core beliefs and your negative mindset and strive toward positive self-esteem, you must become aware of the three basic components of positive self-esteem.

The first is a sense of control and personal responsibility.

We must acknowledge our flaws and mistakes and accept accountability for our actions. You must become aware of your power to choose. You must accept that every action and decision you make will have a consequence for which you alone are responsible and accountable. Every action you take will lead to either success or failure. If it helps you become better, it's a success. Keep that in mind and don't be afraid to make mistakes. If you connect with God and trust yourself, your low self-esteem will transform into a positive one.

The second component is a sense of belonging and acceptance. This means having a positive approach toward life and associating with people who will respect you and have a positive influence on you.

This will enable you to gain a sense of belonging and even love. As a result, you'll feel emotionally secure and more confident. It will start to change your self-concept and self-efficacy, which will positively influence your self-esteem.

The third component is having a sense of competence. This influences your self-efficacy and your ability to accomplish the objectives you strive for in your life. After you start focusing on the first two components, your belief and perception about your level of competence will improve. You stop relying on others and gain more confidence over your own abilities and potential. This helps promote your self-efficacy and self-concept when you accomplish small tasks and gain positive feedback from people who genuinely care about you. The positive feedback communes with your positive attitude to help you recognize your potential and learn to see positive skills in others. None of this can be achieved without putting your faith in God and asking Him for help.

Summary

Your belief plays a crucial role in both good and tough situations. It keeps you grounded. It makes it easier to become aware of the hurt you're doing to yourself with self-talk, and it makes it easier to return to yourself with love.

When life unexpectedly starts to fall apart just when things were finally going your way, this makes you feel frustrated, fearful, and desperate. You are more likely to make bad decisions without thinking clearly, and you end up in more trouble that makes the situation even worse. It's common for a series of bad events to make you feel lonely, lose hope, and stop believing. This happens whenever you forget to ask for help from God for a solution to your problems and to meditate to reflect and think clearly so you'll make sound decisions.

Meditation and reflection is a crucial exercise for cultivating self-love and compassion.

Chapter Review

Don't just jump into situations, no matter how desperate you are. You must learn to sit back, be still, and listen to the small voice in your mind, the one that tells you to do positive things that won't hurt you. Thoughts become reality, and you must learn how to create thoughts that bring positive results. Until you begin to follow the positive, powerful thoughts inside you, you'll always struggle to find success.

Start creating positive thoughts. What are some thoughts you will create? Did you know that you attract what you think of most? What are some of the thoughts of thing you have attracted to yourself in the past two weeks.

Exercise

List any three things that made you happy today.

1.

2.

3.

List five things you're grateful to that God has given you.

1.

2.

3.

4.

5.

List one wish you desire and write down the steps for how to move toward achieving it. You can even draw a picture to visualize your wish.

I trust that everything happens for a
reason., even if we are not wise enough to
see it.

Oprah Winfrey

With everything that has happened
to you, you can either feel sorry for yourself or
treat what has happened as a gift. Everything is
either an opportunity to grow or an obstacle to
keep you from growing. You get to choose.

Wayne W. Dyer

CHAPTER FIVE

My First Marriage—Looking for Stability

I met my first husband when I was twenty-years old, and I
married him at the same age. It was love at first sight. Back then,
I thought it was love, but really, it was attraction at first sight. I
was a pretty, slim, young island woman with dark-chocolate skin.

He was a good-looking mixed American man with a Black American mother and a Caucasian father. His complexion was caramel, and he had beautiful curly hair. We immediately fell in lust.

People ask me often if I married him because I was in deportation, and the answer is yes...and no. No, because I was instantly attracted to his good looks. Yes, because when I got to know him over the following six months we dated, I wouldn't have married someone of his status because of the many things I wasn't familiar with and didn't want to be part of. My main concern was not wanting to be deported to Haiti.

I overlooked his verbal abuse, the instability, and the craziness going on around me. It was a strange relationship, happy one day and miserable the next. I couldn't see that I was creating even more problems in my life than the deportation. Regardless of the situation and despite what was going on in our lives, I married him.

As women, we become very passive and emotional when it comes to nurturing others versus nurturing ourselves. Women always want to save others, because that's what we have learned

from society and are taught in all the images around us. In TV,

newspapers, and magazines, we see women cooking, cleaning,

holding a baby on our hips, and helping the men in our lives.

Recently, the media has begun to promote cougars—old,

more mature women—who better their looks and upgrade their

fashion to attract younger men. I don't agree with that, though

women should be proud of how they look. Such a statement from

the media diminishes one's self-worth. Instead of a woman who

understands her worth and loves herself, this promotes a woman's

desire to do anything to gain a young man's attention. She should

already know she's worth someone who will love her for herself, not

just for her appearance.

I didn't just marry my first husband to avoid deportation. I

came to care for him and love him. I wanted to give him an

opportunity to have a loving family and stable home. Perhaps that

would help him become a good husband a father. I thought, once

we were married and living together, we would be happy. With my

green card, I could attend college and study medicine. Once we were well-established, we could have two kids.

I had big plans, but nothing went the way I thought. Our marriage was a total disaster. I worked long hours to support the family, and I became the sole provider. It was very hard, but I wanted to keep our family together, so I did what I had to do.

I still don't understand why I stayed in that marriage for sixteen years. Many people ask me about it. When your self-esteem is low, and you don't know it, and there's no one to turn to for support, a person often says in that relationship no matter how crazy it is. In those days, despite everything, I felt he was the only one I had. I kept thinking he would change.

Not only did I stay with him, I ended up with four children, all boys. Sadly, my youngest baby died of SIDS (sudden infant death syndrome) at the age of three months. It was a very difficult time for me.

It was tragic for my son to die so young. However, I had to find the strength to go on with my life. When a family member offered to let me move to Florida with her for a fresh start, I quickly accepted.

Symptoms of Positive Self-Esteem

Once you start relying on God and focus on changing your approach toward life by using the components of positive self-esteem instead of feeding your negative thoughts and low self-esteem, you'll be able to acquire the positive traits that are a strong indicator of having positive self-esteem.

It's important to know that you don't need an inflated sense of self-esteem, just a positive one. As mentioned earlier in the components, you must be willing to take responsibility for every decision and step you take. You must acknowledge that every action has consequences, and each one involves a risk. You must be willing to be accountable for your actions and the outcomes they bring. You must be willing to accept your mistakes and limitations and learn from them.

- When you achieve high self-esteem, you begin to recognize your potential and skills and start aspiring toward an aim or objective for your life. You become persistent in striving toward achieving an objective.

- When you acquire high self-esteem, you become genuine while interacting with others. You don't fear being evaluated by others or allow them to influence your self-esteem. You're more capable of being honest with yourself and others.

- With high self-esteem, you have more patience. You're aware that good things take time. You become more tolerant of the limitations in yourself and others. You are willing to accept the flaws in yourself and others and become more willing to forgive yourself and others.

- Those with high self-esteem have strong internal values. They have strong morals and principles that must be followed. When you start to believe in God and ask Him for help, having faith in the Almighty, your sense of direction and energy changes. You start to form a connection with good and finding His inner voice within yourself.

- Those with high self-esteem focus on self-improvement. They wish to better themselves and groom themselves toward excellence. They strive to become better and don't believe in being stagnant in life.

- Those with positive self-esteem avoid dwelling on the negative aspects of life and focus on the positive. When you start to form a connection with God, your entire outlook on life becomes positive. You're more grateful toward others and your own life. You begin to appreciate and focus on the positive aspects of yourself and others, boosting your self-esteem. To work on the components of positive self-esteem and transform your negative self-esteem into something positive, you must acquire certain habits.

- You must eliminate negative thinking and negative self-talk. Stop beating yourself up. If you perceive yourself as negative, others will, too. You must be aware of and acknowledge your limitations while carefully avoiding becoming self-destructive and constantly criticizing yourself. That just escalates your negative self-concept and self-esteem.

- It's important to list your positive attributes and focus on strengthening them, using them to excel. When you focus

more on your positive qualities and aim to improve them,
you acquire more positive self-esteem.

- Learn to identify your self-worth and value yourself. If you
  start giving yourself respect, others will, too. Be aware of
  what you deserve and set limits. Refuse to accept anything
  less than what you're worth. You must make sure that you
  and others know that you deserve respect and love. Don't let
  anyone treat your poorly.

- Be willing to take risks and accept failure. You'll learn from
  your mistakes. Accept that you have flaws like any other
  human being. Don't let failure pull you down. Instead,
  learn from it and become better. Learn to improvise by
  learning from your mistakes.

- Learn to accept rejection. It's important to understand that
  not everyone will like you. You can't please every individual
  you meet in life. Avoid letting rejection influence your self-
  esteem. Don't see it as a failure but as a learning
  opportunity and a sign you're a genuine person.

- Meditation helps you find God's inner voice. You'll be able to find peace by connecting with Him at a higher level. If you keep asking God for help and put your faith in Him, you'll find inner peace, positive self-esteem, and a positive life.

Summary

When you choose to rely on people and forget to believe and trust that God will be your guide, you end up making rash decisions. You're consciously aware that you wish for stability and deserve happiness and a better life, but you end up choosing the same life you had during childhood—a life full of domestic abuse and lack of affection. Your subconscious allows you to devalue yourself and teaches you to accept the idea that you aren't worthy. This leads to more loss and grievances.

God's greatness lives within you.

Tamara Dalton

Chapter Review

Often when you stop loving yourself, you feel trapped by your emotions and hold onto relationships that are no longer meaningful. You get stuck like I did, feeling as if I needed the worst people in my life.

Do you feel trapped by a situation you'd like to let go of? What are some of the things that would happen if you let it go?

What are your plans for change?

Write down the advantages and disadvantages of leaving a bad relationship. Make an action plan and step-by-step program of how to implement it. Tick off each step from your checklist action plan as you complete it.

Respect yourself

And the others will respect you.

It is better to take refuge in the Lord

than to trust in man.

Psalms 118:8

CHAPTER SIX

Moving to Florida for a Change

A family member offered me a chance to live with her in

Florida with the children, when I lived in New York. She advised

me it would be a good idea to start over, as well as being an

opportunity to leave my husband, because our relationship wasn't very good.

What a great idea, I thought.

When we arrived, she welcomed me and hoped I could stay with her and find a better life. Two weeks later, when I hadn't found a job yet and was still broke, she asked me to leave with the children. She said her live-in boyfriend said there were too many people in a one-bedroom apartment.

At midnight, she told me to pack my stuff, get the children, and go. I had to wake them and get them ready without knowing where we would sleep. All I could do was cry with my babies in my arms.

Once again, I believed and trusted in other people instead of God. When you're that far from God's mercy, that's how disorganized your life becomes. I felt I had no one to lean on or turn to for support. There was no one. Just when I thought I was moving away from my husband and starting a new life, I found myself homeless with three small children.

I had no career and no job, though by then I had training in a nursing assistant program and graduated with a certificate.

However, I was just getting settled in Florida. I hadn't transferred my nursing assistant license to Florida yet, so I couldn't find a job. I was petrified, sad, depressed, and lonely. All I could do was cry and try to build up my strength again.

I called a female friend that night. At least, I thought she was a friend.

"How much money do you have?" she asked.

"Seven hundred dollars."

I gave her the money, and she let me rent a nice small house. She said she oversaw renting the house for the owners, and I could stay for a year.

God must have sent her to rescue me, I thought.

The owners of the house came back in three months and kicked me and my three children out of the house. Once again, a friend deceived me. I felt my only choice was to return to my husband, so I made another big mistake. I offered to have him move to Florida with us, so he could help us get back on our feet again. I felt that whatever assistance he might give was better than nothing.

When you have no one to lean on and are ruined spiritually, that's when you don't consider self-love, self-value, or your own needs or worth. Instead, for security, you turn to the only thing you know, no matter how unreliable it might be.

I felt all I had was my husband. At least he would be with us to help with the children. He was a good father, very recreational, taking them to the park and playing games with them. I had to buy a pack of cigarettes for him and give him money to take the kids out, but at least he was there.

When we stop praying, though, all communication with God is lost. If we aren't talking to God, our lives become a mess.

According to Philippians 4:6, *Do not be anxious about anything, but in everything, by prayer and petition, with thanksgiving, present your requests to God.*

I needed God in my life, but the lack of prayer and meditating to God let me go astray. My problems went from bad to worse.

Summary

When you become distant from God, you allow Satan to influence you, which keeps you from making sound decisions. You keep trusting and being dependent on help from other people when you should seek those things from God.

To leave a bad situation, you end up taking a detour into even deeper water. You start drowning in a series of betrayals, mistrust, loneliness, and more wrong decisions.

You become so lost in turmoil that you forget you need to return and ask God for help and guidance. When you become distance from God and stop communicating with Him, it brings even more problems.

Chapter Review

What did I learn from staying with my husband and this experience? Sometimes, you must bite the bullet and give in for a while until you're stable enough to work on your plan. I worked and paid my husband to baby-sit our children. It wasn't what I wanted, but, at the time, he was my only saving grave. I kept planning, working, saving, and getting an education to better my life.

What have you sacrificed to get where you wanted to go? Have you ever been in a situation where you didn't pray, or Satan didn't allow you to pray, because you were so far from God's face?

How did you find the strength to start praying again?

List the ways you can fight the influence and misguidance of Satan. What steps should be taken to move back toward prayer?

What means or resources can you use to come closer to

God?

> To establish true self-esteem, we
> must concentrate on our successes and
> forget about the failures and the negatives
> in our lives.
>
>   Denis Waitley

Don't rely on someone else for your
happiness and self-worth. Only you can
be responsible for that. If you can't love
and respect yourself—no one else will be
able to make that happen. Accept who
you are—completely; the good and the

bad—and make changes as YOU see fit—

not because you think someone else wants

you to be different.

Stacy Charter

CHAPTER SEVEN

Education Was always on My Mind

At least I wasn't totally unaware of where I was in life.

Through it all, I took college courses in nursing. At first, I thought

I wanted to be a psychologist, because I had an interest in the

psyche of the human mind. Psychology fascinated me, because I couldn't understand why my parents were the way they were or why a friend took my last penny when she knew the owner was returning.

I started taking psychology courses at a local university, while working as a nursing assistant at a local nursing home. I fell in love with the patients and the care I gave them. After two years of studying psychology, I decided to change my major to nursing.

I transferred my college credits from Barry University to Adventist University of Health Sciences, formerly known as Florida Hospital College of Health Sciences, a well-known, reputable Adventist university known for its rigorous nursing curriculum. The school helped students perform at a higher level. It was clear from the beginning that a student either succeeded in doing the work, of he or she would be dismissed. I was very fearful of failing, because I saw many young students without children or family responsibilities who were dismissed when they couldn't master the coursework. The situation was scary, as I studied and prepared for the nursing license.

I walked into the classroom, because I didn't have a choice.

I had to pass. My life and my children's livelihoods depended on me.

I graduated from the Adventist University of Health in April, 2008, and I took the registered nurse board exam in September, 2008. Once I passed the Florida state exam, I was honored to be a registered nurse.

With a wonderful career ahead, I could afford to divorce my husband and move on. Instead, however, I decided to talk to him. I gave him an ultimatum that he either got his act together, or I would divorce him. Little did I understand that I couldn't change another person. That person must realize something is wrong in his life and make the changes on his own.

He didn't. After many years of trying without success in our dead-end relationship without any growth, I finally decided to give myself a fresh start. In 2010, I finally divorced my children's father.

I thought I was ready to learn from the past, do better, and focus on myself and my children. I vowed I would get my career, income, and life together once and for all, but I was wrong. Being

single and being a man magnet didn't help. Men always showed
an interest in me, but never for the right reasons. I knew what
they were after and was good at saying, "No." After all, I'd been
married for sixteen years. I wasn't a flirt. I didn't even know how.
I wasn't planning to just settle on anyone. I knew better than to
select the wrong man again. What I didn't know, however, was
that I was a codependent woman.

I was doing fine on my own. I had a nice apartment with my
three boys. I had a great job, and I didn't need financial assistance
from a man. What got me was loneliness. Being alone without a
man in my life got the best of me. I wasn't accustomed to being
alone and began looking for someone. At the time, I wasn't aware
that I suffered from codependency and low self-esteem.

Summary

Education is the most-essential aspect of life that can bring
many changes for you. Choose a career you feel calls to you,
something you enjoy doing. After all the accomplishments people

make, having come so far to overcome their struggles until their lives reach a good place, they are still unable to release feelings of worthlessness. They feel a need for someone to love them despite their successes. Like them, I was still a little girl with low self-esteem.

You develop codependency when you feel the need for love and affection from others. You don't realize that changes need to be brought about in yourself instead of expecting others to change.

I love all who love me. Those who
search for me will surely find me.
Proverbs 8:17

Chapter Review

Having a bachelor's degree in nursing helped me sustain a good life for myself and my children.

How do you feel about education? How much do you value education?

Think about where you are now. Are you satisfied with the way things are?

Has lack of education stopped you from being all you can be?

List the names of people who didn't receive education but, with hard work and perseverance, were able to succeed.

Make an action plan for how you can change your life if you haven't received education. Make a task analysis or break down the plan into small steps for you to achieve.

Twenty years from now you will be

more disappointed by the things you

didn't do than by the ones you did do.

Mark Twain

CHAPTER EIGHT

Second Marriage: Looking for Love Again

Four years after my divorce, I turned to a dating website, as that was the big new thing in those days. I knew a couple of people who met over the Internet and were happily married. Why not me? I posted a profile on a website. Not even minutes later, my message box was full of messages. I was excited. I didn't know who to choose for my first date.

When I had to choose one man from a bunch, of course I chose Mr. Wrong. I picked what I was familiar with. Last time, at least my husband and I were younger, and we had three children. Maybe I could understand how I got it wrong.

Now, however, I was older and wiser, though I would never marry another abuser—no way! I never thought it could happen to me again. I still hadn't learned my lesson. I was doing things my way, not God's way. Without God, nothing will ever be right.

When I met my second husband, he wasn't what I was attracted to physically. He appeared somewhat distant. I noticed that he didn't have much to say. I didn't understand my own thinking, because I preferred people with whom I could communicate and interact. The one thing everyone must be careful of is that when you're with someone for a period of time, he or she grows on you. Of course, he grew on me, and I fell in love with him pretty fast.

We were dating for only two months when he said he was in

love with me. He wanted me to be his wife forever. He explained how he grew up unhappy. All his life, he looked for someone he could be happy with. He explained he had a young child and wasn't with the mother, but they were still on good terms. He wanted to settle down. He said he loved God and wanted us to attend church together.

He told me many things that didn't make sense to me, but I fell for it all. He said he felt I was the one for him. To a codependent woman, even though his story didn't sound that good, the fact that he expressed his need for me felt great.

When you deal with low self-esteem, you also have poor judgment. Because of the low self-esteem, I did things subconsciously, things someone with high self-esteem and self-worth would never do. Once again, I wanted to help another man. I was going to save his life. I wanted to make him happy.

When you're far from God's path, you forget about your Heavenly Father's love for you. You love the fact that someone needs you. Subconsciously, I was desperate enough I didn't want to risk his turning away. He might be the best I could find, my last chance to have the perfect family of my dreams. When you don't see any value in yourself, you look for others to need you, validate you, and be grateful for your help. When he explained the struggles in his life, how things weren't easy for him, plus the fact that he was somewhat sad, I wanted to care for and love him to make him happy, or so I thought.

I never thought I was getting myself into more trouble than my first marriage. Call me crazy, but that's how it was for me. Broken after raising three children, I was still traumatized by my past. Later, I learned from therapy that I was perfect prey for such a man. On the outside, I looked strong and confident, and at times I thought I was. I felt my self-esteem was intact. After all, I had a good job, a great career, and was in school to pursue more nursing degrees. What could be wrong?

William James in 1890 said, "Self-esteem is a fundamental human need, essential for survival, not less essential for survival than emotions such as anger and fear."

If I was living without self-esteem, it was no wonder I fell in love and married a man after knowing him for only four months. I never realized I just married another abuser in every sense of the word. Not only did we marry, but I had his child. There were signs that something was wrong with this person, but I ignored them.

In the second month we were dating, he did a few strange things. Against, I was so consumed in my fantasy, I didn't notice. The delusion of having a nice family life made me pretend nothing was wrong with this guy. Thinking he was just different, I convinced myself to continue with the relationship.

Two months into our relationship, he proposed with a nice diamond ring. Even the way he proposed should have alerted me to potential trouble, but again, I ignored my intuitions to be with him.

"If you don't like the ring," he told me, " we can go to a jewelry store and pick out one to your liking."

"OK."

We went to the store, but he wanted total control of the ring I selected, even though he said I could choose whatever I liked. He became extremely angry when I selected one he didn't like. That should have been a glimpse of his bad side that I noticed before I said, "I do." It was my opportunity to run, but I didn't take it. I was getting even deeper into the relationship, even when I knew something wasn't quite right about that guy.

Two months after we became engaged, I needed surgery for a thyroid disorder. My mother, who lived in Connecticut, wanted to come to be with me. My fiancé insisted she couldn't come, because he was a shy person. He wanted to meet her at another time, not when I had surgery. I knew that didn't sound right, but to please him, I canceled my mother's trip, oblivious to the fact that he wanted to break me and control me.

I became a different person. Once I was outgoing, but I became housebound and secluded. He said I had too many friends, and, if he was going to marry me, he needed to be my only friend. Unbelievably, I agreed and started ignoring the few good friends I had. I lost my best friend, Candy, and never spoke to her again. I changed myself to please that man.

On my surgery day, the plan was for my fiancé to drop me off and have Candy, my best friend at the time, stay with me beforehand. He planned to relieve her when I was in surgery, because she had to work.

He dropped me off at the hospital, and Candy met us there. He claimed he had to go home to change clothes and would return to relieve her. He didn't come back until the surgery was over, which was seven hours later, and Candy missed a workday. He proposed to me in front of the doctors and nurses, one again saying how much he loved me and apologized for being late. By then, I knew I shouldn't marry him.

Filled with pity for him, I wanted to save him from himself. I wanted to show him love and compassion, that I didn't care about what he owned or possessed, or what he didn't have. I was dysfunctional, though I didn't realize it at the time. I felt good that someone needed and valued me. He knew that information about me and used my vulnerability to his advantage.

When we married, I was living in two-bedroom apartment. He asked me to move into his five-bedroom house. As a registered nurse, I wasn't impressed by his big house, because I could afford to buy a nice house that suited my taste if I wanted. I was comfortable as a single person living in an apartment, because I didn't have to cut the grass or be responsible for the responsibilities that came with owning a home.

When a person is that spiritually disconnected to herself, to a higher power, or to the God within, she becomes an empty shell. In my heart, I knew I wasn't going to change him, but once again, I wanted to please and love him instead of putting myself first.

I agreed to move in. When we were alone, this man wanted full control of my life. A great way to arrange that was to have a child. Perhaps he thought I would become more vulnerable and needy, because I had no one to turn to for support.

The first four months of that pregnancy were pure hell. He yelled at me and put me down verbally. He told me no one would want a forty-year-old woman with a baby. Every day, he told me how he owned a house and how lucky I was to have a man with a house. I ignored him, because I finally understood he was dysfunctional. I wasn't going to let him do whatever he pleased. I started to realize our marriage was a big mistake and retaliated by talking back to him.

When he saw he couldn't control me despite the fact I was

pregnant, he began being abusive. He went from verbal abuse to physical. He was furious, because I wouldn't let him control me. He thought, once I was pregnant, I'd let him disrespect me. When I didn't, his dark side emerged.

One night, he started an argument with me about the wedding ring. He said he wanted it back. I told him it was a gift. I added I would file for divorce, and he could see if the judge would let him have it back. Until then, I would keep it.

He came to me in the dark and started hitting my belly. I managed to run from the house, as I dialed 911 on my cell phone. I got in my car, but he opened the door with the remote. I jumped out and ran down the street.

He followed me in his car. I thanked God when the police arrived. A female officer grabbed me in a hug and told me I would be all right. The other officer stopped my husband in his car and arrested him.

After all that drama, I was so damage inside that I wrote a letter to the court on my husband's behalf, asking the judge for my husband's release. He was released, only to return to the house and threaten to burn the place down with me and my children in it.

I called the police again, and he was arrested a second time and jailed for four months. Because I kept writing the judge on my husband's behalf, the prosecutor had no choice but to put my husband on probation instead of a longer prison term, which I thought was fine.

I finally realized something was wrong with me, and I needed help. Sometimes, it's OK to seek outside help for yourself. You don't have to be crazy to need such help, especially if you don't have strong family and community support.

I started therapy and learned that I was a codependent person. With the help of therapy and my strong belief in God, I was able to overcome my nightmare.

As I look back on the drama I went through in that period of my life, I keep wondering what kind of mental and emotional trip I was on to let someone abuse me verbally and physically. When someone has low self-esteem and lives a godless lifestyle, those are the situations he or she encounters. That's why we need God to prevent low self-esteem from ruining our lives.

Why would any woman allow herself to be mistreated and degraded by any man?

Yes! I kid you not! He loves you

that much!

Tamara Dalton

Summary

When you still can't follow God's way, you repeat the same mistakes. Your low self-esteem and codependency lead you to poor judgment and the feeling of being valued by others by seeking love and affection from another man instead of God.

When your conscious mind is out of correlation with your subconscious, you tend to reject the good things that come to you and accept things that are unworthy of you. You allow yourself to be abused and devalue yourself, because you believe that's all you're worth.

Chapter Review

How do you think women can protect themselves from getting caught in the trap of abuse?

How do you think this situation could've been prevented?

List three ways as a parent you can teach your daughters to value and respect themselves, to learn to choose what they are worthy of.

1.

2.

3.

List three ways boys can be taught to respect themselves and girls, treating them with respect and love as equals, and to value their worth.

1.

2.

3.

Getting over a painful experience is
much like crossing monkey bars. You
have to let go at some point in order to
move forward.

C. S. Lewis

Let go.

Coach Tamara

After climbing a great hill, one only
finds that there are many more hills to
climb.

Nelson Mandela

CHAPTER NINE

Low Self-Esteem Leads to Poor Decisions

My second husband and I are divorced. We live separate
lives and have no contact with each other, thanks to the law. Also,
thanks to God for enlightening me and allowing me to wake up to a
place where I found wisdom, self-love, happiness, peace, and
stability. I'm able to move on and forward harmoniously with my

Heavenly Father within me.

How could I let a man torture me so much? Why did I allow him in my life? Why did I get him out of jail by writing to the judge on his behalf?

That's my point about what not loving yourself first and not having high self-esteem and living a godless life does to someone. You become powerless and allow others to control you.

Can a person's self-esteem be so low that she allows others to take full control over her life? The answer is yes. I thought myself as having a high standard of living. I seriously thought losing control of my life couldn't happen to me, not at the age of forty and in a second marriage.

It did happen—twice. My goal for writing this book, the reason I'm here, is to prevent others from having the same thing happen to people's loved ones, their daughters and sisters, and, mostly, to themselves.

There are women around the world who hide in their homes and are afraid of loving themselves. They are abused sexually, physically, mentally, and verbally. A few men have similar experiences, but it's mostly women who are caught in the trap of abuse much more than men, because a man can overpower a woman with his physical strength. A woman must learn how to overpower a man with mental strength if she can't beat him with her physical strength, and that strength can only be found within herself.

Women must stop being so passive, loving, and trusting. A scripture in the Bible mentions men who come after weak-willed women. *They are the kind who worm their way into homes and gain control over gullible women, who are loaded down with sins and are swayed by all kinds of evil desires.* [2 Timothy 3:6, New International Version]

The two men I trusted, loved, cherished, and carried sons for did that to me. I could easily blame my ex-husbands and my parents for their lack of emotional support. However, I blame myself for allowing myself to get into such abusive relationship traps and for not putting God first in my life.

When things don't go their way, most people get angry and blame someone else. Instead, they should stop and think about how to turn the wheel in the opposite direction, because the way they are going isn't the right one.

Buddy Dyer said, "With everything that has happened to you, you can either feel sorry for yourself or treat what has happened to you as a gift. Everything is either an opportunity to grow or an obstacle to keep you from growing. You get to choose. At the end of everything, we remain the mast of our own destiny, but the choice is ours. We need to pause and think how we're going to find our way back to self-love."

In Matthew 7:7, Jesus said, "Ask and it will be given to you; seek and you will find; knock and the door will be opened to you."

So, beloved, if we aren't asking, how can we receive? How will you find yourself during or amid catastrophe, darkness, and loneliness? To change, one needs to start taking responsibility for his or her actions. The way to take responsibility is through self-actualization. How can someone do that?

In life there are always things that don't go well. Sometimes, there is no control over what happens to others. However, we have control over things that are preventable. A person must take control of his or her life to make good decisions and accomplish what he or she wants.

According to Immanuel Kant, enlightenment is man's release from his self-incurred tutelage. Tutelage is man's inability to make use of his understanding without direction from another. Self-incurred is this tutelage when it causes lies, not in lack of reason but in lack of resolution and the courage to use it without direction from another. Each of us must come to self-actualization, the realization or fulfillment of one's talents and potentialities, especially considered as a drive or need present in all.

I woke up. I knew I had to change my life. I spoke with a counselor, because I had to learn about myself, my culture, and my self-esteem. I became not only a registered nurse but a skilled life and stress management coach. I give my time to help others. I attend church regularly. I make new, positive friends. Instead of trying to help men by marrying or dating them, I help people who are in the same situation I was in see a better way and to learn the destructive patterns in their behavior before they wreck their lives. My goal is to help young people and adults avoid wrong turns in life by enlightening them to understand the power of self-awareness and God.

Most people live like zombies. They subconsciously do things that their minds have processed over the years. The way people grew up, their culture, and their religion play a part in the way they deal with life's issues when they arise and are processed through their decision-making faculties.

I woke up, because I found myself on a dead zone, a path of self-destruction. During or Amid the disasters, I found myself and learned to love that person more than the one who was hurting me. I became spiritually awakened and enlightened in that moment.

The enlightenment was the voice of God. He was always within me. I just didn't know how to tap into Him because of the person I was. God called me and knew me, so the devil, being very jealous and the serpent he is, carefully camouflaged and deadly, tried to destroy my life. I couldn't see the devil and didn't understand his destructive ways in people's lives. I was able to change my life by deactivating the old self and reactivating my new self and thought processes.

I was able to change my thought processes, because I made a conscious decision not to continue living a destructive life. I needed to live for my life's purpose, not someone else's. I didn't want to keep investing my love in those who didn't care for it. I was tired of helping those who didn't want to be helped.

First, before allowing others to drop their problems into my life, I realized I needed to invest more time in myself. I had to get to know God by doing, so I found me. I started spending more time with myself, nourishing my soul. Marcus Aurelius stated, "To live happily is an inward power of the soul. We ought to nourish the soul. But first, one needs to have courage, for courage is the very motto of the enlightened."

Our soul is God's power, the higher self within us. It lives inside us and can't be altered. It has always been a part of us, but we need to tap into our God power by nourishing it. When speaking about the soul, though, what do I meant by that?

Some of us understand that change is imperative for our spiritual, emotional, and overall life growth. However, many aren't sure how to attain real life changes or to make them permanent, so we don't return to old habits.

Another problem is that often most of us don't want to believe we're part of an unseen God. It's hard for many to believe that we have access to an invisible power source, one that is not only reachable but something we can use for our greater benefit if we only allow our minds to reprogram from the brainwashing we experienced in our lives. That power source is real and unlimited, especially when you learn how to tap it from within. Your life source, your spirit, the light of God, is within you. When speaking about spirituality, we need to change our perspective of what was taught to us about human life.

A new perspective must come into place to achieve true wisdom. We must be able to try something new and take a risk. If you don't like how you've been living your life, if you feel depressed, stuck, and angry, why not try something different? I was amazed when I realized that all along, I was looking for love and acceptance in all the wrong places. Everything I needed was inside me. I just needed to stop and listen to God's spirit voice within. This positive voice gives me direction in life. I was able to do it by spending more time alone and tapping into my higher self. That helped me find my life purpose and self-redemption to become my true self and be whole again. To be enlightened is to be born again. It's a rebirth of the spiritual life.

You must also be very, very careful when seeking to become enlightened, because certain groups of people will tell you go here or there, or you must do things a certain way.

There's no specific way to find yourself, love, and your spiritual being. If you find a place where you can be in silence for a few minutes each day, you can tap into your positive higher self and to the God within. Make time to meditate on God's Word by reading the Bible daily and reflecting on His Son, Jesus Christ's, words. When you're still, quiet, and meditating, a feeling of peace will ensure you're being guided to your inner love. This process must be and feel positive and invigorating. It will make you feel strong, healthy, and full of energy.

It's all about you and the best way you feel comfortable in the silence within yourself. Take time to invite God into your spare time of solitude to find peace. Without peace of mind, nothing will be fulfilled for the best. When you find peace of mind, you can once again interact with those around you in a better way.

When I'm writing, reading the Bible, coaching, alone in a park looking at the trees, water, and the beautiful sky God created, I feel much closer to Him, and I also feel more love inside myself. If you find something you enjoy doing in silence, such as painting, writing, or walking, you'll become closer to the God within you and your higher self.

> Lord, help me to see myself as You
> see me, so that I can love others as You
> love them.
>
> Tamara Dalton

Summary

Low self-esteem and a Godless life lead to poor decision-making skills. Once you acknowledge and realize that a change needs to occur within yourself, you begin to move in the right direction.

Regardless of your environment and who was the source of your low self-esteem, you need to take responsibility for your actions and accept that consciously or subconsciously, you made poor decisions for yourself. Getting professional help to become more self-aware helps you reach toward the right part and achieve your true calling in life.

Accepting reality and being self-aware of your mistakes, letting go with the help of prayer and meditation, help you reach a higher level of human need for self-actualization.

When you're finally able to listen to your inner voice to connect with God, you will find a sense of peace.

Chapter Review

Find a quiet place where you can sit, be still, and relax. Make it a daily practice of sitting or walking, and let your mind become a blank slate so God the Spirit can enter.

How did that quietness feel? After a few weeks, write down

the changes that happen in your life. Use more paper if you need it. You can even start journaling.

Write down your experiences and feelings each time you spend time alone with yourself.

Design a timetable for meditation and prayers that can be divided into separate slots for each. Next, write down what you felt while contemplating God and from introspection.

After reading the teachings of God, write a few pointers from that and a few of your shortcomings. Next, choose one task or habit you can acquire or change from that list.

> If only you could sense how
> important you are to the lives of those you
> meet; how important you can be to people
> you may never even dream of. There is
> something of yourself that you leave at
> every meeting with another person.
>
> Fred Rogers

Some days, I just turn off my phone

and make the day about God and me.

Tamara Dalton

As our own peace of mind grows, so
the atmosphere around us becomes more
peaceful.

Dalai Lama

When we create harmony in our
minds and hearts, we will find it in our
lives. The inner creates the outers.
Always.

Unknown

CHAPTER TEN

The Spiritual Aspect of Life

Six years ago, when I was first introduced to a meditation class, everyone sat up with straight shoulders, good postures, and breathed carefully in and out. God forbid someone didn't properly inhale and exhale with those breaths.

I felt frustrated, as if I weren't completely enlightened, because I couldn't properly take those deep breaths in and out, never mind sitting with my legs folded under my rear end. I eventually stopped going, which wasn't the best thing to do, but no one told me it was OK just to be there. Just being in the silence or being thankful I was there was enough.

Gratitude goes a long way. If you find it hard to stay still to meditate, or your mind wanders in all directions, simply close your eyes and start thinking, *Thank You, God,* in silence for creating you perfectly. Thank your higher self, your guardian angels, Jesus, and the God within, for they are all one.

Your cultural background has nothing to do with it. We're all children of one God. No matter how you choose to connect with Him, it's fine as long as you seek Him with all your heart. There's only one voice within each of us, the voice of God, and He lives within us. We need only learn how to tap into this God-given power and allow Him to manifest in our soul.

Jesus stated in Ephesians 4:3-6, *Make every effort to keep the unity of Spirit through the bond of peace. There is one body and one Spirit, just as you were called to one hope when you were called; one Lord, one faith, one baptism; one God and Father of all, who is over all and through all and in all.*

To change our lives, not only do we have to let go what has been programmed into us, we also must try something different to change our lives. We have been misguided for so long, we're overwhelmed with fear.

Some of us look everywhere to find happiness, peace, and wisdom, just as I did. I went to different churches and religions for answers with no solution in sight, because when we put ourselves in situations, it's only ourselves who can get us out, using God's help if we call on Him and acknowledge Him as our higher self.

Others visit shamans, psychics, mediums, and hypnotherapists—the list is endless—trying to find inner peace and happiness. All along, we have the key to the door of peace, happiness, and wisdom within ourselves.

Meditation

To move toward self-actualization, meditation helps you find inner peace and become closer to God. Meditation enables you to form a connection with the universe and with God at a higher level and be able to feel and connect with the universe, experiencing it positively. Einstein believed that human beings were part of the universe, which is limited in time and space. Human beings experience thoughts, feelings, and emotions as separate from the rest of their consciousness. He believed that's just a delusion of consciousness. It restricts us from being able to embrace compassion or any creation.

When we're entrapped by delusions due to trauma and low self-esteem, we lack a connection with God. Meditation helps dissolve the illusion of separateness and enables us to feel safe. The more you stay in the practice of meditation, the more it elevates your level of connection with yourself and also with your family, friends, the world around you, and, most importantly, with God. This inculcates safety, compassion, and love within yourself and others. You'll be able to experience the beauty and feel a deeper connection with simple actions like watching a sunset.

You'll be able to connect that with God and yourself in a positive approach. You'll begin to see the beauty in everything, which helps you discover yourself and the inner voice of God within.

While meditating, simply acknowledge your anxiety, low self-esteem, and traumatic experiences, and let them be without analyzing or contemplating the source of the stressful experience. Bring it to awareness of your mind and body, then redirect your focus toward mindful breathing. Feel the sense of the earth below you and everything around you. Reflect over the connection with your surroundings. Let go of all the external stress factors and feel yourself being embraced with love and compassion with God and the earth. Feel yourself being held with love and compassion, then visualize your loved ones held in the same warm embrace.

Contemplate how the earth doesn't exist in a vacuum. Rather, it's connected to a higher power that created the universe, and that all parts of it are interconnected. Create this self-awareness in your mind, body, and soul. This will lead to a feeling of connection with God, the universe, and the people around you. You'll feel a sense of belonging.

Return to a focus on your breathing with a greater connection to the universe and God. This meditation of twenty minutes should be part of your daily routine.

Writing a journal after meditation helps you form greater connectivity with the universe and God. It makes you feel positive and will inculcate self-love, helping you toward positive self-esteem and ways of dealing with your trauma by forming a connection with the universe and God.

You can't give to the world what you
don't have. Be kind to yourself first.

Tamara Dalton

Summary

Learn to meditate in silence and listen to your inner voice. If worldly distractions bother you, begin to show gratitude toward God and whatever good, positive things He has provided you. Thank the Lord in silence.

Gratitude toward God and others goes a long way in helping you attain inner peace. It will help you achieve inner peace and allow God to manifest inside your soul.

> True forgiveness is when you can
> say, "Thank you for that experience."
>
> Oprah

Chapter Review

Sit back, be still, and listen to the small voice inside. Learn how to meditate in the quiet of your inner self to find the answers for your life.

During meditation and quiet time, acknowledge your mistakes and confront your pain. Be self-aware of them.

Next, try to accept reality and focus on the positive things you see around you, where you can observe the miracle of God. Write down or take pictures of all the positive things you see.

Oh, Lord, have mercy on me, for I
have sinned against You.

Nothing in life has happened to you.
It's happened for you. Every
disappointment,. Every wrong. Even
every closed door has helped make you
into who you are.

Joel Osteen

CHAPTER ELEVEN

Surrender, Let Go, Let God, and Move on

The ego causes internal fear. Let go of the ego and fear no more. Only one thing makes a dream impossible to achieve—the fear of failure. According to author Paulo Coelho, who wrote, *We are all human, and we will all experience fear one way or the other.*

However, don't let fear control your life to the extent your purpose deteriorates. The time is now, my friends, to stop being afraid of yourself and your abilities. If I had only known how to use my power within, my true self-worth, and my self-value, I would never have let another human being mistreat and abuse me.

If only I had known how to tap into my higher self and learned how to love myself. If only I had known that all I needed was created inside me before I met my two husbands. Where would I be right now, if I had known that I had full access to the power within me?

We have no control of the past and cannot change it. However, we can use the past to build our future. The past can help shape us and change our lives into what we really want to become.

Not only can we help ourselves reach the success we desire, we can help others learn from our mistakes. These past experiences can guide you to stop making wrong turns. If you're lucky, you hopefully haven't made that many horrible wrong turns like I did. Stay on the road you're headed down, watch your life, and observe the people you let into your world. Get your life in order by getting your soul purpose in order. Stay productive not only for yourself but also for humanity.

Today, I'm sitting at home happily and peacefully. I can only wonder, *If I had known the secrets of self-love and self-awareness all this time, where would I be right now?* I would have definitely accomplished my life's purpose much quicker.

I'm spiritually and physically on a higher level of awareness, and it feels good. I'm now living my life's purpose, and my new life is wholesome. I'm listening to the voice, the God within me. My higher self is speaking to me, and I hear it clearly.

I allow myself to shut down and get quiet, to be at peace within. I consciously choose to raise my self-esteem to a higher level, because I know my self-worth. I have become more dependent on myself and don't rely on the opinions of others. I don't follow others. I don't let them lead me where I don't want to follow.

I'm in control of me. I can hear my inner self shouting, "Stop! Stop!" when something is wrong or if something doesn't feel right in a situation. Now I can hear that small voice inside that says, "I'm here for you, if you'll just turn to me." When you wake up to your spiritual self, you'll realize an internal voice is speaking to you and guiding you, just like I did.

To wake up, however, you must first acknowledge there is a path in your life you want to take. You must be able to admit the current path you're on is or isn't working for you, or you need better directions for the path you have chosen.

If necessary, admit you need to change your life's direction to follow a new path. If you don't know what you want, meditate in a quiet place, do your research, and pray until the right idea/path comes to mind. Then you can get into action and follow the path successfully.

Sounds simple, right? Not quite. If it were that simple, most of us would never have taken wrong turns in the first place. To wake up your God-given spirit inside and find the direction to your life path, you must be ready to understand that your worth more than what you've been receiving from life.

That's just a little food for thought. If your life is miserable, it's because you chose to make it that way, no matter if you decided consciously or subconsciously. You chose the circumstances where you are in this very moment. To change your circumstances, you must change your thoughts and the path you're on.

Many choose to stay asleep. They choose the path of self-destruction and won't work through change. Such people don't want to confront their inner pain and suffering. They continue living in pain by living a lie about themselves and where they're going.

One day, everything crashes down on their lives. Only then do they ask, "Why me?" They should have turned to the source within to gain strength, knowledge, and power to find the right path for their lives. That's why it's so important not to continue ignoring the small voice inside. That is God's voice trying to speak to you.

Begin to change that destructive habit by starting to practice not carrying your hurt, anger, and guilt, or your obsessive, self-destructive behaviors. Most of all, don't blame someone else for your actions. You're the only one who can control what you do and what you let others do to you. You have to say, "No. I won't let someone else control my life." Take back your power no matter how hard it is to fight off those who want to take your power and use it for themselves.

God gave you your life for you to use, not for another human being to have control over you, and his or her own life, too. Stop letting other people use and abuse you!

I realized I was being hurt and used by others. In that moment of realization, extreme grief changed to extreme clarity. I knew I needed to make drastic changes in my life. I also realized my life wasn't over yet, and it was time to stop acting like it was the end of my world. I began living like my life had just begun, and I felt an amazing feeling of joy and release.

First of all, my mind was ready to change and live life to the fullest. Most of all, I was ready to be happy. For me, it took a catastrophic incident with my second husband to make me change my direction and salvage my soul into a sincere awakening. I knew I needed drastic change. In that moment of extreme sadness, grief, and excruciating inner pain, I found myself and entered peace of mind. There was no doubt within me.

Stop and think about where you are in your life. What will it take to make you change your life?

By opening my mind, I began salvaging my soul. I knew if I was breathing and healthy, I would not only change but would take full control and responsibility for my life. I married the two men in my life, because I thought I could save their souls by treating them better than I treated myself.

They weren't ready to save their own souls. I couldn't help them. I didn't realize that at the time, and that was why I chose two wrong men to share my life with. I allowed then into my life even when I knew they weren't trying to change their lives to become more spiritual and abundant. You must be careful who you let into your life, because that person may not share your path.

I married a second time without God's approval, because I was a codependent woman. I felt worthless. I thought of myself as weak, a woman who didn't think anything of herself and didn't know her true worth. My brain sent out signals, but my life was so full of despair, it was cluttered and closed.

When you're finally able to see your life patterns and disagree with the outcomes, sooner or later, the mind and heart eventually come together to awaken the inner self to its higher potential. First, though, you must be aware of your journey. I was able to wake up, because I didn't like the negativities in my life. I woke up when I acknowledged that wasn't how I wanted to keep living.

Especially as a hospice nurse, I realized we are all dying. I needed to live for today as if it were my last minute, second, or day. I didn't want to make any more excuses. You also have to make the choice to live your life today.

> When you are at peace with yourself
> and love yourself, it's virtually impossible
> to do things to yourself that are
> destructive.
>
> Wayne W. Dyer

Summary

Your ego, past, and fear of failure won't allow you to succeed. Listen to your inner voice and meditate with God in silence. It will help you understand that you aren't defined by other people's opinions. Be conscious of who you choose to interact with and tell yourself that you're worth more than what you are receiving.

Be in control of yourself and have the willingness and ability to change yourself. When you're ready to change, with meditation and following God, you will be able to change your thoughts, which will help you modify your circumstances. This will prevent you from self-destruction and help connect your heart and mind with each other.

Chapter Review

What can you do to begin the process of salvaging your soul? When will you begin to find the still, small voice inside to help guide and direct your path?

Write down a valuable lesson you learned today in your life and another one from reading the prayer book or through communicating directly with God.

To acquire wisdom is to love oneself;

people who cherish understanding will

prosper.

Proverbs 19:8

So then faith cometh by hearing,

and hearing by the word of God.

Romans 10:17

CHAPTER TWELVE

Quest for Happiness

Multitudes of people around the world are searching for happiness. Many are looking to be enlightened by something or someone. They don't know how to change, and they're sick of the way things have been taught to them or with continuing their lives.

Some restlessly seek peace of mind, wholeness, self-love, and the higher self.

However, their minds have been washed out by teachings that aren't based on the truth and reality of God's Word. According to 2 Peter 1:3, from the *New Living Translation Bible,* by His divine power, God gave us everything we need to live a godly life. We have received all this by coming to know Him, the One who called us to Himself by means of His marvelous glory and excellence.

Without this understanding, people are left lonely and sad, feeling as if something were missing from the inside out.

People don't know how to attain this spiritual awakening. Many times they misinterpret what enlightenment is about. Some don't believe in God. Others don't understand how Jesus could make the statement that He is God. Some would rather believe in any one of the hundreds of deities that have been worshipped for centuries instead of believing in the God within themselves.

A spirit power inside your human body leads and guides you every day if you will only stop, listen, and allow it. The secret of attracting this power is being revealed to you through this book. You just must practice using it to change your life like I did. I'm no different from you, except I started putting God first. He was able to show me His path to self-love, freedom, and peace.

One way to start is to realize there's got to be a way to truly live life to the fullest. There's a place inside you where nothing in this world can affect your soul. In this place there are no worries, and you can blossom with happiness whether you're living alone or not. This power, called enlightenment, comes when you get clarification about who you are and where you're headed in life.

To understand how to use this powerful gift, one must start by first practicing the Tamara's Three R's—rewind, release, and reprogram—and your inner power. You have to learn how to release the content from the brain that has been stored inside your mind. This is information you've been taught all your life. Now it's time to find and connect with your own higher self, the God within each of us.

During or Amid my life's most-difficult time, I began developing Tamara's Three R's. They revealed the lies, brainwashing, and fear that had been implanted in my mind.

The content about when we were born, growing up, and our life history is stored in the mind. Most of us can't remember back that far. I didn't say all of us can't, because some do remember when they were born. As more parents are being awakened and refuse to allow their children to go through what they experienced in life without being properly instructed about the God within us, they ensure their children are well-informed on the subject to achieve greatness in a world full of disappointments and self-hate.

According to American-born spiritual teacher Adyashanti, if you aren't aware of who you are, enlightenment has to do with embracing reality, then escaping from it. Once we embrace reality, everything else becomes easy, and we don't see impossibilities, imperfections, fear, and powerlessness. Instead, we see only greatness within ourselves, and we feel and see only the positive in everything instead of the negative.

I found myself, happiness, and peace of mind. There's so much humanitarian work for me to do in the world. If I'm still breathing and remain healthy, I'll work to help others become

whole again. If I died today, I can honestly say that I lived well.
The past is the past. Today, I'm happy. I'm living my life positively
to the fullest, and nothing in this world can shake me or deter me
from my newfound path of greatness. You, too, can find this path,
but the choice is yours. Good luck!

> Stop being a victim. Take a stand
> and be a survivor.
>
> Tamara Dalton

Summary

You must achieve enlightenment by embracing reality and
being at peace with it, by looking toward only the good and positive
in life. To achieve such a high order of inner peace and a close
connection with God, you must Rewind, Release, and Reprogram.

Rewind and return to your past and recall all the hurt, fear,
and pain. Come to terms with it by letting go and venting out,
releasing all that was in the past by being aware of it and not

allowing it to influence your present. When you release all that was in the past, you take back the power. It awakens your spiritual mind, enabling you to change yourself and reprogram your life in a different way.

For this purpose, you need to meditate and talk to God, thinking of what you choose for yourself. What is your calling in life, and what path do you want to take?

Chapter Review

How will you practice embracing enlightenment and change?

Write down all your past and present history that has been taught to you and now controls you.

List a few small, specific goals you wish to have in different aspects of your future life. How would you want your new version of life to look?

It is necessary to help others, not

only in our prayers, but in our daily lives.

Dalai Lama

BONUS WORKBOOK

Tamara's Three R's Program:

Rewind, Release, Reprogram

Now that you have an idea about your life's purpose, what can you do with it to be happy and to be of service to others?

You're no longer an aimless wanderer; you're now ready to

make good decisions to change your life. You're ready to make dreams come true, to be free and spread the seed of positive living to others. There is no more confusion about where to live, whom to date, whom to be friends with, whom to make a family with.

The career you've always wanted is yours to attain, and you'll excel in it. The promotions you have always wanted will be at your fingertips. You'll know how to behave, when to speak, and when to remain silent. Life decisions in all aspects of your life will become easier to make and keep.

Did you find a new perspective for your life now that you know what you want? Write down your perspective, meditate on it, and process it until it becomes your reality.

Have your mistakes become clearer? It's OK to laugh at yourself. I did. Now that your thought processes are clear, and you're focused, I'm sure you'll have trouble believing the mistakes you made. The good news is, you'll never make them again.

Are you worried about becoming a new person? That's OK. You won't become a different person, but you're so enlightened that you see things for what they are. Others see you as a threat and make you think you're becoming a new person. However, just accept your newfound self while staying humble as new knowledge begins pouring into your mind.

The process of knowing who you are and standing up for that person to become authentic and genuine to yourself isn't easy. It becomes easier once you allow the process to flow and transform you life. There are many steps to take. Now that you've read this book, don't just finish it and feel happy for me. I want you to experience your own life transformation as you begin meditating, taking notes, and completing this workbook.

Let's begin with Tamara's Three R's

> Battered, beaten, knocked down,
>
> abused, neglected, scared, left bruised,
>
> hurt, shocked, surprised, disappointed,
>
> broke, unloved, unwanted, abandoned,
>
> the lowest of lows, rock bottom.
>
> Revitalized.
>
> Tamara Dalton

Chapter Summaries

Chapter One

Family environment and healthy relationships between parents and the whole family are essential for proper self-development of children. Parents must learn to display affection to their children and have open communication with them. They should be able to treat each other with mutual respect. Parents' affection for each other and display of their love for their children inculcates self-esteem, good intrapersonal and interpersonal skills, and the confidence and courage to be aware of their self-worth. The children value themselves and accept nothing less than what they are worthy of.

Chapter Two

Social unrest in someone's country and witnessing atrocities like acts of terror and domestic violence leave an emotional scar and traumatize people. A mother can have a strong influence over a child's life, demonstrating a strong lesson by how she carries out her life. Children learn that she'll do anything to give them a good life despite her own shortcomings.

Nevertheless, lack of presence and/or displays of affection from the mother and an indifferent father leave children with a lack of self-esteem. A household must have family entertainment, and parents must allow their children to express their feelings without fear of being reprimanded. Parents must conceal their indifference from the children.

When children don't receive such an environment, they subconsciously learn to choose the same kind of people, lifestyle, and environment as adults. Those become their own mistakes, but they were caused by learning at a subliminal level that they are unworthy, based on their childhood memories.

Chapter Three

At times, the greatest suffering brings a great opportunity to start a new life. When one door closes and another opens, we must learn to identify when the right opportunity comes along and then take it in the best way possible. Focus on doing the best in what life has provided while remembering your roots and the struggles you overcame to reach where you are. Learn to be flexible and adapt to new environments. This helps you survive the storms and changes that come.

Chapter Four

We plan our lives, unaware that God may have planned something else for us that we don't understand. We see it as an obstacle that has ruined our lives, creating fear, anger, and frustration. Instead of believing and trusting in God, you go into a state of confusion and desperation. This leads to poor decisions and lifestyle choices, because your judgment is clouded without meditation. You dig yourself a bigger hole.

Chapter Five

Low self-esteem leads to selecting the wrong person to marry, especially when you do it for the wrong reasons. Getting married because you're infatuated or to get yourself out of trouble creates disaster and a catastrophic ending. You learn to ignore the signs and signals telling you that it's the wrong choice. One of the reasons for acceptance of abuse and low self-esteem is not just unhealthy family environment or bad childhood.

The ideology and concepts created by social media and other environmental factors about who women are and what they should be identified with, as well as the role they must take, teaches women from a very young age to be objectified and subservient toward men. Learning such concepts enables men to abuse women, and females allow and accept it. Many abused women end up in bad marriages for years, not realizing they don't need another person or a man to survive.

Chapter Six

When you put God in last and become distant from Him, Satan overpowers your thoughts and clouds your judgment and your perceptions about circumstances. You end up relying on and trusting people rather than talking to God and praying to Him for help. You have more emotional turmoil and betrayal from friends and relatives, bringing chaos to your life. You're in the same vicious cycle, back at square one.

Chapter Seven

If you have a plan in mind for changing your life and commit to educating yourself into what you love and enjoy doing, you can accomplish it with enough hard work. The problem is when women have low self-esteem, even if they accomplish a good career, enough money, and a sense of financial security, they still may believe that having a man in their life is needed because of codependency.

After a time, women realize they need to change the situation and themselves, because others won't change. They take the leap and make the changes, finding peace, security, a career, and happy children, but they still feel empty and have the need for a man or a sense of love and affection in their lives. They have become codependent and still aren't connected to God.

Chapter Eight

Lack of communication with God and meditation maintains low self-esteem and codependent needs for validating oneself by being wanted and loved by others, instead of seeking love and validation from God. It leads women to end up with the same kind of abusive man after ignoring all the warning signs. Women repeat their mistakes, because they aren't following God's way to make things right. This brings more depression, isolation, and abuse until the point where officials become involved.

Chapter Nine

When someone hits the breaking point and realizes she needs to change, she begins to understand that her mistakes came from poor decisions. The moment a woman accepts and takes responsibility for her actions, becoming aware of her mistakes and acknowledging them, she begins moving in the right direction.

Accepting professional help like therapy and meditation will assist the healing process. They help you shut down the sounds of the inner and outer thoughts and hear the actual voice that helps you communicate with God and reach a level of self-actualization.

Chapter Ten

Show gratitude to every individual. It goes a long way. When meditation still brings distractions, all you need to do is be silent and say, "Thank You, God." Allow God to manifest in your soul, so you can achieve self-actualization.

Chapter Eleven

Don't let your ego or fear of failure get the best of you. Internal fear makes it impossible to manifest your dreams. You need to tap your inner voice and meditate, telling yourself you aren't defined by what people think of you, and that you're in control of yourself.

By bringing heart and mind into harmony and following God's way, you can remove self-destructive habits and change your thoughts, so you aren't influenced by others. Positive thoughts will change your circumstances. Tell yourself that you're worth more than what you receive in life. You'll start to see all that is good and positive in life and will learn to ignore the negative.

Chapter Twelve

We all want happiness, self-love, and inner peace. The way to receive enlightenment and acquire self-actualization is through meditation and tapping the inner voice of God. For this you need to follow Tamara's Three R's—Rewind, Release, and Reprogram.

Recall childhood memories and confront your pain. Accept

reality and release it to focus on the good in life. Change your outlook and focus on your goals, and you'll begin to see all the positive, good things in life, observing God in everything.

Understanding Self-Actualization

When you practice mindful breathing and meditation, you're better able to cope with traumatic experiences and realize your self-worth, moving toward positive self-esteem. When you have positive self-esteem, you can form positive connections with others and become more aware of your worth and value. You'll see everything around you with a positive outlook and greater connection with God, which allows you to reach self-actualization.

Abraham Maslow believed that humans have few basic needs. Only when they can satisfy those needs will they be able to reach the level of self-actualization.   When you begin to feel positive and have better self-esteem and a greater connection with yourself and others, you'll be better able to satisfy those needs. According to Maslow, to acquire self-actualization, you must first satisfy your physiological, safety, love, belonging, and self-esteem needs.

When you practice meditation, mindful breathing, and work on attaining positive self-concept and self-esteem, these help you work toward achieving a high level of self-actualization.

Self-actualization means being self-aware of your limitations and potentials. You'll be able to utilize your positive attributes and potentials to the maximum. You'll rise above the materialistic and worldly needs and be able to reach who you are meant to be in the universe. You'll be able to achieve your goals and will be more grateful toward life, more accepting of yourself and others. This leads you toward a greater connection with God.

Attributes of a Self-Actualized Individual

People who achieve self-actualization are not only aware of their flaws and skills but can accept such things in themselves and others. They associate with positive people, accepting them for who they are and form a deeper connection and relationship with others on a more-positive level of communication.

As they become more enlightened and form a greater connection with God, they can perceive reality as it is in any given situation. They become aware of themselves and others from a realistic perspective. They have a deeper sense of empathy and compassion, with a greater sense of purpose of what they wish to accomplish. Their level of gratitude and ability to help others, their ability to find inner peace and a connection with God, make them feel a strong sense of happiness. Self-actualized individuals are motivated by growth and are more grateful with a greater sense of purpose to help others and a desire to keep growing toward excellence.

Self-actualized individuals can perceive the bigger picture and are humbler. They're also able to resist the temptation of worldly desires and the stereotyped culture of society to look beyond manmade norms and values. Becoming famous or having money no longer gives them happiness, but being able to pursue their dreams and become what God intended them to be gives a true sense of happiness.

Their positive self-esteem and having other needs satisfied helps them acquire a strong connection with people and the universe to become self-actualized. This enables them to form connections with God and find the inner voice of the powerful being within themselves.

Self-actualization is also practiced in humanistic and positive psychology and is used for person-centered therapy.

When you're able to acquire a positive self-concept and positive self-esteem, it leads you toward the path of self-actualization. You become self-aware of your skills and abilities, utilizing them to become what you're meant to be, but that only comes with mindfulness.

You achieve mindfulness and greater connection with God. With His help, you're able to reach your destination and explore your life journey by finding your true purpose in life, what you're meant to be in this world. Your positive energy sends out signals to the universe, and your connection with God allows you to achieve self-actualization and inner peace. This leads you toward your quest for happiness.

Paulo Coelho believes when you work toward becoming who you want to be in life, the whole universe conspires to help you achieve it. This can be done only when you let go of your fear and form a greater connection with God.

Four Steps to Greatness in Finding Your Life's Purpose

Tamara's Three R's—rewind, release, and reprogram— change our brain contents from what we've been told to be true.

Rewind—Take a few minutes to take a deep breath, inhale, and exhale. Think about what you've been taught all your life that causes you fear. It can be fear of the unknown or fear to make decisions which leaves you emotionally paralyzed.

Release—Once you have acknowledged these things, take a deep breath. Inhale and exhale them from your system for good and say, "Today, I release fear and negativities from my life. I am [state your name], not my parents. Today I choose to live my life's purpose to the fullest."

Reprogram—You're ready to reprogram your mind set. It's

not easy to reprogram yourself within. All the contents you have learned weren't absorbed overnight. They were done by watching, seeing, and by being taught to you. As you stay aware of the Three R's, detoxing your life, you'll continue to replace the brainwashing, negativity, and fears with thoughts like, *I am good. I'm worth it. I'm me. I'm authentic and genuine. I can do and be anything if I put my mind to it and live my life's purpose to its fullest.*

Step 1: Tamara's Three R's

How will you rewind, release, and reprogram your life?

Notes:

Step 2: Identify Your Life Themes

What Is Your Great Dream to Achieve?

Find out what you really love or what you'd love to do.

Forget whether you'll make money doing it. Just do it. Go for it without hesitation.

Notes:

Step 3: What Is the Meaning of Your Life?

Find the meaning behind your life theme. Why do you love it so much? Write down your reasons with a smile and start thinking about how it's no longer a dream but something you'll turn into reality.

Notes:

Step 4: Make a Bold Statement about Your Newfound,

Exciting Life Purpose

Make a bold statement about your newfound, exciting life purpose. Start talking about it. Give it momentum. Explore it. Meet others who have the same interest. Talk to those who are like-minded. Read positive books like this one.

Now you're ready to live and die happily, because you found your life purpose and found yourself. Go on—live, love, and laugh to the fullest.

Summary

Now that you have acknowledged your mistaken reality and are in connection with God, you can finally see life from a different perspective. Use that to help change your career, relationships and love life. Meditate and pray on how you'll focus to achieve what you dream of becoming or having.

The Three R's are like detoxification that doesn't happen

overnight. Practice your breathing exercises and state positively that you aren't a failure. You're more worthy, not like someone from your past. Choose a certain aspect of life to focus on. Pray and meditate on that and find meaning to your life.

Explore your new choices by talking about people with the same dreams and aspirations. Take risks and meet positive people. Read self-help books that will help you achieve your goals.

> Blessed is the one who finds
> wisdom, and the one who gets
> understanding, for the gain from her is
> better than gain from silver and her profit
> better than gold. She is more precious
> than jewels, and nothing you desire can
> compare with her. Long life is in her right
> hand; in her left hand are riches and
> honor. Her ways are ways of
> pleasantness, and all her paths are peace.
>
> Proverbs 3:13-18

I am exceedingly afflicted; Revive
me, O Lord, according to Your word.

Psalm 119:107

We are afflicted in every way, but
not crushed; perplexed, but not driven to
despair; persecuted, but not forsaken;
struck down, but not destroyed.

2 Corinthians 4:8-9

ABOUT THE AUTHOR

Tamara Dalton, a Registered Nurse and spiritual life coach, shares her personal story in *The Love Within,* and will enlighten you through lessons learned about the Power of God within us, self-awareness, self-discovery, and self-love

Tamara shares how she was able to rebuild her life after

domestic abuse and poor life choices to create high self-esteem from the inside out.

The Love Within will inspire you to change the way you let others use and control your life. You'll learn how to put God first in your life to find "the love within," to develop strength and abilities from your secret divine power within yourself. The goal is to search within yourself to find your purpose in life to be whole.

Life can get hard when you're driving on the wrong road. For me, it was searching to find a positive lifestyle. However, I kept falling back into the same old negative relationships and patterns with people who weren't going in the same direction I wanted to follow.

During one of the darkest times in my life, I discovered the secret that inspired me and helped revitalize my life. The small voice inside saved me and brought me to the light.

I wrote this book for others to share the experience, knowledge, and wisdom I learned after taking those wrong turns.

https://www.facebook.com/coachtamaradalton

It is far greater to acknowledge the
flaws within yourself than to criticize the
shortcomings of others.

Tamara Dalton

www.ingramcontent.com/pod-product-compliance
Lightning Source LLC
Chambersburg PA
CBHW060252050426

42448CB00009B/1624